They Go

Mark DeBord

BookLeaf Publishing

Seasons Come and They Go © 2022 Mark DeBord

All rights reserved.

No part of this publication may be reproduced, stored in a retrieval system, or transmitted, in any form or by any means, electronic, mechanical, photocopying, recording or otherwise, without the prior written permission of the presenters.

Mark DeBord asserts the moral right to be identified as author of this work.

Presentation by *BookLeaf Publishing*

Web: www.bookleafpub.com

E-mail: info@bookleafpub.com

ISBN: 978-93-95784-61-0

First edition 2022

DEDICATION

For Mom, Dad, and Rob. I miss you all and I love you.

ACKNOWLEDGEMENT

Lisa, you are the love of my life. My best friend, my inspiration, my everything. I love you.

The Seasons

The spring of my life
Didn't begin
Until you came into it

I know it will lead
Into many
Summer days and nights

And,
As the changes of fall come,
I know our love won't.

Because, during the winter,
When everything seems
Cold and dreary,

We'll have each other
… and that is all we need.

Today Is The Day

Today is the day
You can use in a way
That is a step in the right
Direction

You can start
Acting the part
So in the mirror you like your
Reflection

The things that you say
And the way that you play
Have an impact on people's
Affection

So take that small step
Don't be scared
That it must be
Perfection

We can all do our part and
Think with our heart
And finally make a
Connection

Mark The Second

Mark the second
On the face of your watch
When inspiration strikes.
Hear the bells chime.

Mark the second
Time that it happens.
And realize that
It happens all the time.

Mark the second
On the face of your watch
When hope appears.
See the stars shine.

Mark the second
Time that it happens.
And realize that
Hope is yours and hope is mine.

Mark the second
On the face of your watch
When the smile shows through.
Feel the warmth in your heart.

Mark the second
Time that it happens.
And realize that
Love resembles art.

Beautiful, but different
In each of us.
Mark the second
It happens to you.

The Tree

The tree lost its leaves, the limbs are all bare
From the cold and the wind, the rain and the wear
From the strain of the weight the trunk had to bear
It bent and it swayed, no more shade under there

As the damage was done, and the sun shone through
And the warmth and the light came right into view
The seeds fell to the ground, dug deep in the soil
They rooted and searched, and started to toil

Rigid and gray, so near to death
The tree stands alone, holding its breath
Till the season is over and life rears its head
In the midst of the branches lifeless and dead

Seasons come and they go
But the tree holds its ground

If it waits long enough
New life will be found

A Glorious Sight

Today I saw a hummingbird resting on a branch.
What a glorious sight,
Since by nature they seem to be
In continuous flight.

Its tiny body barely
Flexing the branch.
Its beak like a needle,
Hard to see at first glance.

How lucky was I to witness this bird.
Oblivious to me; as sometimes I am to the world.

Spring Cleaning

Tis the first day of Spring.
A time for fresh starts,
And new beginnings.

A time for change,
And metamorphosis
Like caterpillars into butterflies.

A time for cleaning out
Our closets and our minds.
Becoming beautiful again.

No matter our situations
Or mind frames,
A new day is dawning.
And, with it, new
Opportunity for growth.

Spring cleaning.
A new beginning for all.

Whatcha Thinkin'?

Thoughts run through my head.
Endless. Seamless. Random.
Sometimes I can see them.
Like static electricity in a pitch black room.

They continue.
Nothing fits into a category.
All jumbled up together like fruitcake.
Who eats that, anyway?

Whatcha thinkin'?...
What? Huh?
A seam; in place between thoughts and speech.
The flow stops.

...Uh, nothin'.

What am I scared of?
That I won't be heard?
That what I think isn't important?
Or worse yet, stupid?

Back to my thoughts.
Something new has gained my attention.
Endless. Seamless. Random.
I can see them again.

Whatcha thinkin'?…
What? Huh?
A seam; in place between thoughts and speech.
The flow stops.

Hmm. Nothin'.
Just random stuff.
Always. Nothing.

Love Haiku

It's a love story
This thing we have between us
I'm in love with you

You are the reason
My life has joy and meaning
Today and always

Not gone a day yet
My beautiful on my mind
Always in my heart

In Memory

Lots of smiles and a whole lot of laughs
Early mornings and bike rides
Football, baseball, and
Country road car rides

Late night chats
And lessons learned
Farm fields planted
And wood fires burned

Small town men
With big time hearts
Rich but not wealthy
At home where it starts

Down by the river
Or out at the lake
On a bank or in a boat
Fishin' stories were made

Respecting our elders
And making them proud
Knew when to be quiet
And when to be loud

Humble and simple
Try not to judge
Live and let live
Life's hard enough

I can see those faces
Grins ear to ear
Cherished memories
From all of our years

Gonna miss those smiles
And remember those laughs
Look to you for wisdom
As all the days pass

Time heals all wounds
I'm not sure if it's true
But I'll keep moving forward
As you'd want me to do.

Monsoon

Dust and darkness, flashes of light
Wind shakes the trees
Rain, hail, flying debris
A random occurrence, unpredictable
Destructive, chaotic, beautiful
Life is created through the cycle
The seeds are watered, the roots are fed
New life comes and old life restored
Disaster to creation in short order
Mother Nature using the desert as a canvas
Bringing color where there was none
And creating life where there was death
Just a storm. You can let it pass you by
Or you can appreciate the beauty
Of the dust and the darkness

Flushed by Footsteps

A covey of quail flushed by footsteps
In short flight, spreading, expanding outward
Then, back together as the danger passed
Dispersed and then rejoined

Nature imitates humanity, or is it the opposite
Fear initiates reaction, comfort reels back in

A mother quail leads her chicks
In a line across the road, weaving
Their feet a blur of sticks as they hurry
To the nest or foraging for food

Mothers prepare their children for life
With a hope they spread their wings, and return

A constant struggle.
Simultaneously letting go and holding on
Expanding, contracting
A covey of quail flushed by footsteps

Winter

Winter.
Cold and dreary
Bleak and weary
Frost on grass
Chill in the air
A coat
And hat
Scarf
And gloves
Rosy cheeks
And frozen toes
Glossy eyes
And red nose
Blanket of snow
Ice on trees
A grey sky
Winter freeze
Clean, pristine
A Time for soup
And hot chocolate
Blankets and friends

Away

Distance draws us closer
Despite the miles between
Missing the comfort
Of your presence
And the calm

Anticipation of a return
Like being next in line
Excitement for what is to come
The satisfaction of being
In your arms again

Distance draws us closer
But the hurt is there
During the moments I wish I could share
And the times I feel alone
Apart but still connected

Age Is a Number

Throw caution to the wind
The whole world in front of you
Years lie ahead
They seem infinite
Then, one day
They aren't

The flick of a switch
A new perspective on life
Wisdom of experience
Brings a new approach
Then, one day
It isn't

In the rear view mirror
Memories of the past
Closer than they appear
Farther than you'd like
Then, one day
They aren't

Changing

Changing colors
Falling leaves
Falling temperatures
Changing season
Falling stars
Falling rain
Changing perspective
Falling expectations
Falling desires
Changing attitude
Falling
Changing
Everything changing

Sunrise

What a way to start a day
Orange fills the sky
Creeping over the horizon
Bringing light to the new day

Streaks across the skyline
Awakening the world
A dove chirps, a lizard scurries
Jackrabbits hop away

Startled by the feet
Of a man who just wants a glimpse
Who needs the connection
To nature and serenity

A mile or two in his mind drifts
Away from the daily grind
The division and complaints
Put aside for just a moment

Quail flush, a coyote howls in the distance
The sun is full now, the desert awake
His mind is clear, ready for the day
Sunrise. Another opportunity awaits

Obstacles

Life is in front of you
With goals and dreams
Wants and desires
All yours for the taking

The destination straight in front of you
But the road is deceiving
Twists and turns
Hills and valleys

Let it stop you or push through
Let it define you or don't
It's up to you, you have control
All yours for the taking

What we expect and what happens
Are often very different, but it's up to us
To decide if we learn from the
Hills and valleys

On to Something Else

The thoughts come quickly
But are gone in a moment
On to something else
Something shiny
A distraction
Focus
Back on track
Something nice
On to something else
But it's gone in a moment
The thoughts come quickly
The thoughts are clear
But then they're not
Doubt sets in
Cloudy
Hazy
Back on track
Something important
An idea, a revelation, hope
A never ending stream of thought
As always, the thoughts come quickly

CPSIA information can be obtained
at www.ICGtesting.com
Printed in the USA
BVHW050900140623
665885BV00014B/1322

9 789395 784610